Night Talk
and
Other Poems

Richard Pevear

Night Talk

and Other Poems

PRINCETON UNIVERSITY PRESS
Princeton, New Jersey

Copyright © 1977 by Princeton University Press

Published by Princeton University Press, Princeton, New Jersey
In the United Kingdom: Princeton University Press, Guildford, Surrey

All Rights Reserved

Library of Congress Cataloging in Publication Data will
be found on the last printed page of this book

Publication of this book has been aided by a grant from
the Paul Mellon Fund of Princeton University Press

This book has been composed in VIP Palatino

Printed in the United States of America
by Princeton University Press, Princeton, New Jersey

Designed by Laury A. Egan

CONTENTS

PART I

PART II

ACKNOWLEDGMENTS

The following poems were first published, some in slightly different form or with other titles, in: *The Hudson Review* (Energy, Speech, For a Political Prisoner, Summer and the Sorgue, Wild Asters, Summer Storm, The Beautiful Acceptance, Mnemosyne, Motion and Rest, Little Acmeist Elegy, Waiting. "Quiet night . . ." Prehistory); *The Nation* (Talisman); *Boundary 2* (Epilogue); *New Directions 34* (Les Illuminés, The City, Two Russian Goat Songs, Building as Farming, Auberge de Peyrebeilhe).

PART I

To Autumn

We've lived through another year of war,
A blood-wet spring, an incendiary summer,
A prodigal spending of lives, spirits flown
Like these leaves blown crosswise in the wind.
And the strange nature of our harvest is
To arrive here year after year with empty hands
Although we've sown living seeds in the dark earth.
Empty hands, gesture of the recurring question
The dead have died for and fled into your arms.

Double Labor

"The aim of life is not a state of mind but
Some form of activity." But your great labor
Is building impenetrable states of mind
With consummate cleverness, out of your fear
Of exposure. Hands do not fashion for the eye's
Delight, eyes do not see what the hands do,
Which always means murder. You've quarried your defenses
Out of the earth, now you sit in your own made
Darkness, essentially cut off, in your praises
Assuming the light and will of heaven.
The wind which is time, the rain
Which scatters the light of morning, don't touch you.
Nevertheless, traveling at high speed,
You spin out a makeshift series of inventions,
Excuses, anything to turn your eyes
From the inevitable, head-on crash against the wall
Whose perfect construction I am celebrating.

Energy

As though the center of the sun were everywhere
An instant unfolding, in the sudden light
There is a great deal of movement
Which looks like

Men in bronze armor marching on a city, like
Women in chains, like walls building up,
And an explosion, and people
Searching in the ruins.

The signal fires meaning Troy has fallen
Sow their salt ashes in the mouths of the dead.
At the heart of numberless embraces
It is already cooler.

Speech

These are words without a fable, without music,
Awkward when they try to speak of love, which is seldom,
Bitter when they point a finger at some injustice,
Half-aware of the unthreaded labyrinth of action.
A wooden facsimile of the perfect language
Heard for a moment and lost, vainly sought for,
Although it sings calmly in the air, the earth, the water.
These are words that would clothe the simplest object
In its own simplicity, but twisted from their purpose
They burn on your tongue like an acid penny.
Words which, yet, if you face them squarely,
Yield a hard light and, being inadequate,
Leave space enough for the world to flow into.

Lykaon

The morning was beautiful, sunlight
Danced on the river water, but
By afternoon the fisherman
Had caught too many fish. Towards evening
The sun lay belly up, swollen and gassy,
The air was unbreathable.

Now there are tears in the summer house.
Helen weeps over Hektor's body
For Helen. Achilles weeps for Patroklos
Who was a better man

Than you were, foolish Lykaon,
Playing naked in the river
When there was a war on.

For a Political Prisoner

Lord, if energy is eternal delight,
What of the uncounted dead who have gone down
Empty into death like husks of seeds?
High up the sun burns over the fields, it
Sees nothing and is perfectly just,
And whoever walks in the spell of its light
Between earth and sky is a man by all laws.
Lord, I put down these words to recall
Those gone under, helpless to save
The flame of their lives, and to speak of a prisoner
Locked at the bars of his narrow window
All night watching for the features of your love
Across the dark hold of space they talk of conquering.

The Gardener

to Alain

There is more order and the order more visible
In cultivated fields than in free nature.
I don't make the order, I make it appear.
One day my flesh will turn the color of this earth,
My veins choke with roots, my eyes sprout lilies,
Between my hands and the ordainer of things
Perfectly blue sky, perfectly green trees.

Summer and the Sorgue

for René Char

In the Sorgue up to his waist, at the parting of the waters,
A man with a long peeled pole with a scythe-blade at the end
Dips sideways in the water cutting loose from the bottom
The long water grass. On the bank
There are two young men, a woman asleep at a table,
Three empty benches, and you and I.
There is a water wheel fixed to the stone wall at our left
Uselessly turning its heavy moss-covered paddles
And three clean replacements. In the water
The grass-cutter cuts long swaths of bright green grass
And lets them drift off downstream slowly with the current.
It's the time of vacations. The sun alone takes up
Its heavy labor in the fields, which may seem
Miraculous, uncalled-for, but we are the more deceived.

Wild Asters

Now come the asters, purple, unclenching like fists.
The fall rains bring them on, there is something about them
Of springlike, sudden and awkward. Asters resist
The early frosts, the fields would be desolate without them

And we be resigned to winter, having no choice.
In the sun they turn white and look like first snow
Or a white animal half gone out of sight. Giving voice
To the turning weather, the geese fly south. Asters don't know

Or are not afraid that time has turned against
Their naive love, lays waste, that down the skies
The sun slants more and more away, moment by moment
Light lessens, things die: the asters stand staring like eyes.

Return of the Light

Soon after dawn begins a trickling of water,
Black pools under trees, the year wakes up
With reflections of leafed-over light, treetops
Washed in the bright sky.

He still sleeps in his winter and suffers
A thousandth dream of war, his heart
Brims over with blood, time thunders to a
Stop: birds in the trees!

I swear I have always loved you, I have never
Betrayed you in my thoughts, if I cry
I don't know you, the reason is beginning
To dawn on both of us.

I don't know what's happening or how to gather
My care to offer it to a new day.
The sound of moving water carries off within me
My monotonous hopes.

There's nothing left. I can only open to you
Like an eye and wonder, how blessed it is!
The sun is fire and fire a destroyer, but
For us it is light.

Summer Storm

The wind blows heavily, the trees all together
Bend and sway like mourning women,
The two-months burnt-out air is dampened with
A foretaste of rain,

Darkened with clouds. And the sky breaks open,
The dust is hammered black, the flowers
Snap from their long stems, the trees wail and
Throw down their leaves.

You might have grown utterly silent, withdrawn
From the world's illusion, as the world
Withholds itself, body and color, through the long
Droughts of summer.

You might have moved into perfect seclusion,
Turned inward, gesture of refusal,
Sipping from a hidden spring, your own darkness,
Poisonous water.

The rain beats everything down. I imagine
It blew like this on Golgotha the day
Before black Saturday, or is that an image
Out of early painting—

The bent figures huddled together, the wind,
The beaten hillside? Let it happen.
The storm is truer than your private, plaintive,
Dissevering sorrow.

The trees shed dust, shed leaves, shed hiding.
More is going on, as usual, than you know.
They sway distinctly against the on-driven
Encompassing sky.

The Beautiful Acceptance

Glory to those who are not afraid of disaster,
Who at the uncertain moment will place all they have won
In hazard, aware that the odds are only human
Despite successes

And that, as Mallarmé said, one throw of the dice
Will not abolish chance. Pyrrhus, when he saw
The street grow narrow behind him, the gateway blocked,
Fresh reinforcements

Struggling in to help him when he wanted
To retreat, the alien city alarmed,
Attacking from every direction, his own men
Wounding each other—

A nightmare worse than his worst dreams—
Did not look around for a bargaining position,
For the necessary betrayal, for a quick abdication.
Knowing nothing

Of the enormous veneration of life and property,
Considering the fall of cities and kings
Glorious, he took off his crown and rode out
Into the enemy.

The beautiful acceptance of the unavoidable,
When history takes on flesh and becomes an ambush,
To give off life as fire gives off light,
Consumed at the limits,

Asking for nothing but by a bitter insistence
To overcome shame with straightness of heart, refusing
All consolations: the world at any moment
May become translucent.

Mnemosyne

In the quiet afternoon
The birds still sing, for them there is no
Catastrophe. Thinking of you
I see the faces of hothouse flowers
Staring through glass at the frozen world.

All those faces are yours, you are crowded
Like history, but unlike history you look for
Moments of stillness and as time pulls forward
You pull back.
What you love is the grass springing out in the morning,
The night and its stars.

Because we are your flesh, our condition
Is suffering for you.
We act in the world that was young once but
Our souls drift out on the dark river
Fateless, uncollected
And go down.

Only you will be able to tell our story,
Not for us but perhaps
In the place we have left behind, our homeland
Still in the light of your unappearance.

Motion and Rest

When the maenads murdered and dismembered Orpheus
Because he refused their god and preached Helios
Apollo from the Thracian hill and spoke against
Ritual killing,

His limbs were scattered but they threw his head
Into the river Hebrus and as it drifted down
The long stream, through mountainous country, uncut
Cedars and hemlocks,

Sheer outcrops, thickets tangled with ivy,
Banks where the blue-flag iris blossomed,
Where moss-deer shadowed the water, the head of
Orpheus, singing

Toward Lesbos, held out in a constant moment
All that he was: his song recounted
Animal enchantments, the inner force rising
In trees like fountains,

The sweetness of the flesh, the stunned silence
Of the gods of death, the impossible consent,
The steep return, the bitter struggle with
Himself and the negative

Pull back down from the sun-filled cave-mouth
To eternal darkness. The flowing water
Was transparent as his song and although it took him
Into unknown country,

Altered times, though it threatened to silence
His forecast on disenchanted rocks, Orpheus
Sang in the lips of his song and his music was
Glamorous, charming,

Unreflective as the cedars and hemlocks, the sheer
Outcrops caught in sunlight, the banks
Where the blue-flag iris blossoms and moss-deer
Shadow the water.

Little Acmeist Elegy

Gone under snow
The hillside, its young green, its dry
Blond curls of summer, flowers under sky
Of the apple tree, driven below.

Snowdrifts. A blast of wind breaks
Across the black water, the hulking animal
Storm, blind in its dead weight, takes
All day to fall.

But then at night the watcher sees
A last change under the eye
Of the moon, under stars that nudge into the sky
Like white, hibernal bees.

Waiting

Suspended animation,
Between heartbeat and heartbeat.
A polar bear like a frozen breath
Curled up in the snow asleep.
Between the no-longer and the not-yet,
Dust motionless
In sunlight caught in a window,
Bellini's St. Francis
About to receive the stigmata.

Offering

for three friends

After you left the fog returned
Blowing across the harbor.
For three days it has hung in the spiky
Branches of the pines and the brier-roses
Are fading in the salt wind.
In my mind I stroll through the underworld
Gathering the colors of beach peas,
The lime green of waves breaking over black rocks,
The strong purple of common vetch,
To bring your shades to life.

Les Illuminés

Ice fields polished by wind
From the mountains behind us,
The frozen ocean ahead, the glare
Of a thin heatless light
Not sun enough
To resurrect the finally dead.
Between here and Kolyma
There is no measurable distance,
From '38 to now
No accountable time. If change is
Motion or mutation, the wind
Is changeless, disembodied, an unmoving
Force exerted equally over
The totality of matter.
On the map the baby face puffs
Its cheeks, the official
Deploys his troops,
New lines of power along old borders.
Not on the map, the small
Fire, the circle of faces touched
By its troubled light.

The City

The city, which labor has raised up, stone
In fountaining arcades, shelters more
Than the builders imagined: moments or sudden
Glimpses of past life,

Their own acts caught in the high traceries.
The architect's blind geometry; birds come
To nest there, martin and swift, their songs
Drift down the roofed air

But fly back again at night as stars seen
To move by a great law—dance, the first sketch
Of the dance floor; place, word, image: history
Roars through the streets,

Up above, balconies and oriels
Guard a strict silence, like the nameless dead,
Like soldiers who obeyed and were buried under
The stone at Thermopylae

Whose silence says, "We have no interest
In these momentary survivors and their obscure fate.
We rest in the gathering place like
Water in a well."

In the same way, even to ruins, the birds
Return, the flowering vines cling, the bees
Thrive in rough hollows, in perfect chambers
Deposit their honey.

Talisman

A last thread of river slips under the bridge
Out towards the mouth of the harbor,
Where rocks give back rumors of deeper water,
A signal! a white arm waving
From the far edge of sight. What is left here
The fish crows inherit. In the emptied light
I study the structure of a seashell, whorled
Out of its lost beginning, and the seed
Your talisman, final reduction of the flower,
Round, hard, and purposely flawed

Prehistory

1.

Baked like a shepherd's pie, full of flowers
The watery green meadow against the black green
Of the pine woods, the ocherous shade.
And two horses grazing—
Wild mustard, marsh grass, fallen apples,
Their taut bellies all breath, emptiness—
Above them a flight
Of fish crows, embers of the house
That burned last winter against the sky,
And I can no longer
Find a place for my memory
Of the woman who lived there alone, reduced
To ashes in the cellar-oven. Fruit sometimes
Ripens too quickly in the fire,
And nothing is gathered in.
And that is a sign. But what more
Can ever be said? On islands
In the northern ocean, not only
On islands but on the northernmost
Tips of the islands, on the sea-cliffs
Walled off to the south, turning away from
That human story, the bedesmen
Built their waiting-houses—
Grass-filled, gathering
Richness in the ground, their strung stones
Told over and over on the lips
Of the island horses. Not lost
But as if asleep, the horses
Move into an almost classical distance,
Into August, into the rift, the calm eye
Of the unreaped meadow. But to abide
Is to be forever expectant.

2.

White days of March, so much is lost
And so much withheld.
The sky is blank, suspended, the sea-mist
Questions the presence of trees,
Their dark indifference to the weather,
Wave after wave blowing through the branches.
Of days of thaw and days of freezing,
The ridged and rutted
Memory of too many pointless acts,
The road has forgotten everything it knew.
Spring has come like Schliemann,
Who broke into the treasury of the Mycenaeans
Looking for gold and splashed around
Knee-deep in the wet clay of layer upon layer
Of tablets, the bankbook of the deadly kings.

3.

Sunrise, an open window.
The curtains are blown aside.
The trees hung up for winter
Against the wall of the sky
Shake out at the surprise
Of warm air. In the scaffolding
Bits of drab green, goldfinches,
Carpenters of this moment.

Carpenters building
A summer house on the rocks
By the edge of the water, return
To work, abstractly. The sea is quiet.
The men are drunk with possession,
The turpentine of fresh wood.

Two Russian Goat Songs

1. INTOXICATION

for Andrei Amalrik

A dark drink of mud and crushed leaves
In water holes after the squall, the year's end
Comes suddenly, small rain from the sky,
Immense rain from the trees.

Open on all sides to the light now,
There are no more secrets.
Nothing is happening now but
What you see.

No divination in these pools.
Yeasted with earth, black decay
Works at the parings of a rich season.
This is the god's sign: lightness of view

And the heavy breath of the earth. Imagine
What futures the Romans argued for themselves
In the fifth century. In the sixth
Century goats are grazing in the Forum.

2. THE MONUMENT AT KUIBYSHEV TRANSIT PRISON

So Eden appears,
The same scene taken into
The notched eyes of goats,
The round eyes of children.
But the woman, shading
Her eyes, one hour
And then two hours,
Scarcely moving, saw
Prison and death
Below the green hill.

Three kinds of innocence:
The innocence of sleep,
The innocence of waking,
The innocence of knowing,
Looked into the dark
Of meaningless affliction.

The woman stood
In a hard wind,
A cloudy summer day,
An hour, two hours,
A hand raised, an arm,
A great strain of wings
Broken, broken
And so completed.

This is the monument
Set up for his comrades
By one prisoner
Who looked back, there
Where there is no monument
But the long hill,
The perdurable goats.

Epilogue

One breath of words to praise
The Russian poet's goats,
Those icons of persistence,
Though they stripped of green
The hills of all mankind
In Tuscany and Greece:
They are the river's water—

Enduringly interchangeable,
Tuneless bells that dinned
The ear of Dionysius;
The end of Stalin's terror
And of all demonic worlds
Is in their spermy stink
And milky heaviness.

Provisional Ode

I

The god may have envied the dead killer
Disemboweled in the dust, abandoned to dogs,
More than he pitied the immortal horses.
Lacking that, he was the shadow of a shadow.

The faithful wife told a truer story
Unraveling each day's weaving at night
Than the one about her faithfulness. Yet
That was true too. Where there's no certainty

There should at least be music. If I try
To see the end clearly, I'm lost in foreshadowings,
Grateful but wandering. My pencil makes
A milky line. Print blackens it.

II

Something in the time's air makes me neglect
The small garden of my own mortality,
Leads me to play the ecclesiast. The sun says,
"What is for you is new, a small garden

Whose law is my law and your law, in fact is
The law." Lethe, who will carry my shade
In its frail boat over to the place of shades,
Is it that concealment, which waits for me,

Does not wait for what my eye lights on?
I want to walk, merely, through sun and shadow
With my useless freedom—useless unless
Or until they try to take it away.

III

This life, a small garden, yet more spacious
Than lasting: prehistory under my feet
And the advance of air over all that moves
Through it. "The present, which is with us

Eternity" (Claudel). "The small round floor
That makes us passionate" (Alighieri).
The weakness of loved things is in love,
Praiseworthy, as long as the talk continues.

IV

And now I see you, finally, and can speak:
A sudden spring of words in the desert
Of my mouth. That is only an image of you
In my speech, my speech in your being.

In Exile

"If no such path leads back to Florence,
I will never enter Florence again. . . . . "

Pondering, somewhat adrift: place, weather,
Seasons, friends, health changing

But not the one resolve that became him.
This too is exile, resolved, into the open

Under stars, the sky's mirror, pondering the same
Sweet truths, adrift in the same night. . . .

And I know how the sightful man wants blindness:
Florence! bread without allegory.

Building as Farming

The purposeless branches
Of my attention,
A bird somewhere in them
And in the bird's beak

A seed of the music
To retune the stones.
Anonymity hides
What labor reveals.

The hierarchical
Moment goes quickly
But leaves the ground turned up
And staggered with light.

Auberge de Peyrebeilhe

Station to station, swallowing
Humble dust, clear water:
We are all on the same way
Though not by some law together.
But you, my scattered companions,
How faint your letters are,
What poor warmth they offer
In a cold month, on a hard bed,
In a strange house. What should have been
Would have been stronger, drawn
To a final meeting and the tongues of flame.
Rain above the tree line, I remember
A skull of stone, and the last road ends
In air, and happening onto
The Auberge de Peyrebeilhe where travelers
Were murdered in their sleep.

Balin le Savage

1. "CI-GÎT ... "

His time was bounded by two faultless errors,
The taking of the fatal sword
And the final combat, the two great brothers
Resolved in their one blood.

There are trees, and an open meadow in summer,
Silent, hypnotized into
A simulacrum of presence, with a slight
Wateriness at the edges,

And the requisite clash of battle, as noiseless
As harmless, because the curse
Is what kills and it has killed already
In unknowable foretime.

And yet the other, his clear double, struggled
In Balin for life. He said,
"Me repenteth that ever I came into this kingdom
But cannot turn now again

For shame, and what adventure shall fall to me
I will take." To his last act
As his first he went clothed in the strange radiance
Of human contingency.

2. THE DOLOROUS BLOW

Why should that king have been the protector
Of the ill one lying in the inner chamber,
Rich array, cloth-of-gold, the four pillars
Of silver upholding a clean gold table,
The spear lying on it, strangely wrought, marvelous?
Chivalry, the inoperative ideal, drove Balin
To the heart of the alien. There he confronted
His insolent, sworn enemy
In King Pellam's mess hall and with his dark sword
Clove him from skull to breastbone, Garlon,
Who turned out to be the king's brother.
The hall rose against him. Balin, sword broken,
Searching through all parts of the castle
For a weapon, naturally burst in there.
The king hot behind him, and hesitating only
A moment in awe of the room and its occupant,
The shimmering light, took up the spear
That had drawn the last mortal blood from Christ's body,
Turned and drove it into Pellam.
Death struck the castle and the cities around it
And blighted the land. Later, riding out
Of that country, he was asked by some that survived,
"Who are you?" And he said,
"My name is Balin le Savage." And they said,
"Woe to you, Balin, who struck the dolorous blow."

A Romanesque Carving

Basilique St. Andoche, Saulieu

The angel is always there.
The ass sees that, Balaam does not.
For him recognition is an issue.
Between them he is a blank and should be
A mediation, the word-catcher
Fails to catch the important word.
And the more he resembles the rocks,
The vineyard walls, mute pasture,
The closer she comes to a human nature,
Rising as he sinks down
Into the blind sea of matter.
Unbearably close at last, she will speak.
And his eyes will be opened
To the drawn sword, the angel, himself
Included in the order
That leads to that taut right arm.
The blessing will fall on him
Like a stone in water.

PART II

You lie back in bed with all the abandon
Of a summer's field sensing the sun's warmth at dawn,
Alive with particular life—
Dew streaming on the grass, unbending.
A breath of wind stirring, and within it all
The archaic smile of the meeting
Between dark ground and sunlight
Little by little
You have become my thought's substance or color:
From clouds fleshed in the last light
The brightness of your body drenches my eyes
Like a gust of rain against a window.

A harvest of our days together:
Dust of grain-threshing in the window light
Burnishing the air,
Odors of wheat and heat and sweet grasses
Cut early, damp hours drying in the sun.

No becoming or passing away but a whole world
Lowered into my memory. Oh
Those days! the tall grain of those hours!

Still Life

There are apples in the cupboard and a bowl of almonds,
Glass dishes (one with a chipped edge), cups, wine bottles,
Plates, linen folded in squares.
The apples and almonds sleep in their closed, full shapes.
The dishes and linens have forgotten being set out or unfolded.
The apples have filled the cupboard with apple-smell,
Dusky and sweet when I open the door.
I am not keeping track of the days you have been gone.
They are all one day.

Quiet night. Rain falls through the leaves like birdshot.
The woods drink up shower after shower, drink up
The showers and the silence between showers. I imagine
Nothing is left.

Sleep, dream, however far it takes you
From the one who lies here.
Simply the whisper of your breath sustains me.

For You, from Elsewhere

In me there are two: the one
Makes a profession of agreement
And would like, like Oedipus, to say
All is well. To the other it is all
A fatality. They are inseparable.
The first may be right, beyond
Our bodily functions I have little
Contact with him. The second is demanding
And does to my endless explanations
What water does to salt. I have been
Elsewhere for more than one day.
The fire burns down in the grate
But the sky brightens. On the wall
I've written out the riddle of the fleas
That made a fool of Homer:
All that I've seen and grasped
I've left behind,
All that I've not seen and grasped
I bring with me.

I remember an afternoon
And you were sleeping.
I saw your kindness then,
Your folded wings,

The strain gone out of you
Of being always
About to fly off, your long
Form the two banks

Of a river, and time flowed
Through you then,
Endlessly repeating itself
In your stillness.

Not the long winters, the isolation,
Waves driven onto the rocks all night
By the north wind, but their image in my eyes
Turned you from me with a broken word.

Where are the bright-feathered ones that stir
New life up with their cries, the lovers,
The blind ones? Have I let them all
Fly back into the dark unspoken?

Dazed from too much black coffee
The mind imagines clarity, the longed-for
Action beside Skamander; raft, storm,
Shipwreck, a cold bath, Leukothea. . . .

A domed hive, wax of days,
And my thoughts are bees.
But song is no more certain
Than remembrance—

On wet days yielding to water,
On dry nights scattered among
Stars in the flawed sky. Secret
Increment of

A selfless labor, I would wish
For more than the little needed
For the time when the measuring cold
Comes finally

And the stilled lips lie apart,
Perhaps only one name if it
Gathers into itself both
Token and warmth.

Midsummer night, Titania,
The clouds have changed the moon
Into that other moon, worn thin
By time to an airy thinness,
Lucent gold behind
The night-mist. All our talk
Was only a way of reaching
The silence we have drunk
From each other, the speech of lips
And hands. Titania, I think,
But call you Leukothea.

In a Country House

We climbed up to the small room
Under the eaves, a thin roof between us
And the moonless midsummer dark, we brought
A small light with us

That burned, burned all night by the window,
But we didn't think of anyone who
Might steer by it: we were inside it,
It was inside us.

And though the time passed, we were not
Aware of where we had come to, only
That we had come together, and so
The time passed. At dawn

We heard voices on the balcony under
Our window, like two fools from Chelm
Each proclaiming his highest virtue—
The one color-blind,

The other tone-deaf. What untrue
Truth possesssed them both! All colors
Seem to be one on a midsummer night
And all music love's.

Almond eyes of the Shulamite
I said, not knowing it was your name!
Dark months had come before you
Through the same door. The words

Had burnt out on my tongue.
I slept. Yet something was awake
Inside me, and my lips moved
To say the forgotten, unguessed. . . .

Time has been rich with us
But hard, what it gave it set
A term to. Our green bed
Is another's field. The watchman

Sees what we do, his order
Is already given, yet it might be
At least that he finds you
Looking for me, not looking away

And you ask him, Have you seen
The one I was with? I would not
Set a seal on your heart.
Love is strong as death, jealousy

Cruel as the grave. I have
No house, who will condemn me then
For giving what I have? My lips
Move to say the forgotten, unguessed:

Return, return, O Shulamite,
That I may look upon you, let me
See your eyes again that
Changed my ashen song to praise.

I looked in your eyes and heard
My own call echo
Down the sides of a well: bird,
Heart, where did you go?

Not-to-be-held. A star
Melts there, otherwise
Nothing to say how far
You've gone, to what other skies.

You, Here?

When her father's daughter went under
And her lover joined her, and her fate,
The world was a stone in her hands:
Pain, roughness, and weight.

Your way of loving and not loving,
Of being, like an echo, elsewhere,
Of yielding but giving nothing,
Is like holding air.

I don't blame you, or understand.
Something persistent in me
Confronts with a solider land
This ghost-ridden city.

From the Old Welsh

Rain falls, the streets are wet,
People hurry to each other or
Away from each other through the half-light.
I don't go, my wound will not let me.

Long will be the night, vacant the city,
Starless the sky and the sliding river,
Time's envy gone from the voice that says
There will be rain tomorrow.

La Beale Isode

They didn't have to know each other
To know what their first meeting would come
To mean for them, what it meant already.
Their eyes saw, their lips spoke.
Afterwards they could spend long hours
Together telling the common fable
Of their earlier lives. The wordless
Promise of their first words came
More from flesh and bone than thought,
More from touch than memory.
It was the gift they never took back.
The immediate, full acceptance of
What lives in another. The story goes on
Endlessly, intricate, in ways absurd,
But you are with me when I think
Of them, and the figure lets me tell you
Something, as when Isode says,
"For Tristram suffereth great pain for me
And I for him," we glimpse that love
They never think of escaping from.

The Stars Again

for L.

I said I didn't blame you: that
Was a lofty pose, meant to be true,
Inwardly what I struggled for.
But those long nights alone, you
Throwing yourself around the city
Not to come back to the familiar
That oppressed you with its voices more
Than strangeness and silence me—
My attempts to reach back, half-drunk
Phone calls to other people elsewhere,
Useless reasoning, worse self-pity,
Became a kind of blame. I made
A myth against your absence, praising
Antigone, her father's daughter,
The one I wouldn't name, and no one
Understood it. Like all myth-makers,
Seeking the deadly aim of power,
I found it aiming me. Power
Was not what I wanted, or surrender,
Or the embrace of shades, but this
Speech in the open space between us,
The night sky above the river.

The change I had foreseen
And refused so long, you brought me
With your certain hands
And in your anonymous eyes
Where I've read so many names.
My love for you is a wound
And a threshold. From behind me
The light of daybreak no longer
Reaches, the way ahead
Waits in the light of evening.

December 24, 1976

Votre âme pour que j'y sois
Mon absence était nécessaire. . . .
—Paul Claudel

You've taken your eyes away
And your intelligent hands
Are working somewhere else.
What are a few days?
And yet it seems that time
Has stopped in my narrow room.

This holiday no one sings.
I think of the child abandoned
As a man and of his last
Perforated cry.
The wind blows where it will,
The cold comes in on us all.

And I think of your least gesture
Multiplied in the depths
Of a past that you don't see
Because you are its eyes,
That I can only look into
When I look at you.

So the Greek woman waited
Beyond hope for a sign,
The sun's hesitation
Comes on the longest night,
Absence calls for presence,
Snow for a single crow.

The Visit

You came when I least expected it
And offered what I no longer thought of,
A spirit but suddenly a woman speaking
Your foreign tongue with pure directness.
Chance to you is a destiny, you
Seem to know something very important
About me, and are not afraid.
You say what you bring is above all pain.
But I've loved another woman too deeply
To turn away from earthly sadness,
Slept with her, our bodies warmed
And wound in desperate estrangement,
And cannot find the word to say
That would save me and not save her.

Night Talk

If you kiss me and turn away
And when I ask you if you love me
Your hands answer but the words
Die in your mouth, I am surprised

At my own unconcern. Unseen
The stars come out above the city,
The unsaid is a caught breath
Between us: all is, nothing moves.

Over the obvious obsession
That holds these buildings up and that
Will also bring them down, the stars
Come out. Our heads together, lips

Close in the eyeless dark, we say
Dangerous things and nothing matters
But our laughter and the stars
That burn unnoticed in the sky.

LIBRARY OF CONGRESS CATALOGING
IN PUBLICATION DATA

Pevear, Richard, 1943-
  Night talk and other poems.

  (Princeton series of contemporary poets)
  I.   Title.
PS3566.E9N5   811'.5'4   77-2533
ISBN 0-691-06347-8
ISBN 0-691-01342-X pbk.